Black History is also

Loving Vs. Virginia

Virginia may be "for lovers," but in 1957 it was not for Loving

The racist laws that prohibited interracial marriage and the long history of the fight against them is best told by the almost fairytale love story of the Richard and Mildred Loving. Complex legal arguments are reduced into plain language - empowering the reader to understand how the fight to defend human rights continues today.

Richard and Mildred did enjoy a fairytale romance - at first. As children, their families were close friends and the marriage and birth of their children were celebrated as bringing everyone together as one big happy family. But then, at 2am one night, the Sheriff stormed their home and arrested both of them in bed, charging them with felonies. Facing prison, they accepted exile from Virginia. When they began to dearly miss their families, and wanted their kids to know their grandparents, and go home again, they were forced to fight for their freedom, paving the way to keep other families safe, too.

© 2023
by Aaron Brachfeld
Edited by Brandy Combs
ISBN: 9798394980732

Table of Contents

1957 Virginia may be "for lovers" but not for Loving
    What are Racist Laws?
    Love Birds to Jail Birds

1958: Loving to Fight
    Exile from Virginia
    Precedents: the History of Challenging Interracial
Marriage Laws

1967: Free Lovings
    Victory
    Happily Ever After...Eventually
    Interracial Marriage Rate Increased
    Same Sex Marriage
    The Loving Legacy

Appendix: the United Nations Declaration of Human Rights

1957 Virginia may be "for lovers" but not for Loving

What are Racist Laws?

Mildred and Richard Loving both grew up in Caroline County, Virginia. At the time, most of Virginia strictly adhered to racist laws - though their town of Central Point had never really paid attention to these sorts of laws.

What are racist laws? Racist laws are those which assign people a "race," and assigns each race different rights and responsibilities.

"Race" is a word in biology that means "subspecies."

While science has always known there is only one, single human race, racists disregard science. Instead, they believe there are multiple races, and that some people are not quite human.

And so, racist laws are based on the idea that some races are superior, and others inferior, that some people are better than others, more deserving of freedom, rights, wealth, opportunities and resources, and that some people do not deserve these things.

In fact, racists believed that some people were so much less than humans that they were no different than domestic animals.

Racism led to the mass enslavement and subjugation of billions of people, and horrific human rights abuses against them in that enslavement - because those perpetrating these crimes did not understand these "inferior races" as human at all, but merely animals.

Ironically, animals were sometimes treated better than these people racists understood to be inferior. This was because the racists not only thought some of these so-called inferior races were less than people, but hated them too, and thought some were like domestic animals - and others were like pests and vermin.

They called all these other races "Colored." Though there is no strict definition of what "White" actually is (Europe has always been ethnically diverse, with large populations of indigenous Asiatic, Arab, Semitic, and Sub-saharan peoples, among others), "White" was generally understood to be Anglo-Saxon, Germanic or otherwise Western European in nature.

When the United States sought to end racist laws and slavery, the Southern States (including Virginia) rebelled and fought a war to preserve their right to enslave and control these so-called inferior races. Their economies depended upon the slave labor of Blacks, but also there were beliefs that if these people were freed, especially the vermin races, they would harm White people - like feral animals might.

There was also fear that "interbreeding" would occur, bringing an end to the purity of the "superior" White race.

Consequently, the rule of "one drop of blood" was adopted: if a White person had even a single ancestor who was Colored, they would be understood to be Colored under the racist laws.

However, not every community in the South believed in this nonsense, and did not have racist laws. And it is important to remember that quite a few communities outside the South did. And still do. The fact that these Southern States rebelled and fought a war to defend their racist ideas should not be held against all their residents, many of whom bravely resisted and fought against their local rebellious governments against racism.

One of these communities that never became too concerned with the fallacies of racist laws was the town of Central Point, which had always been a mixed-race community.

Love Birds to Jail Birds

Mildred's family was of mixed ancestry: she was Rappahannock, Cherokee, Portuguese and Black, but identified as Black. On her arrest affidavit, the Sheriff had identified her as "Indian." Richard's family were White. The Lovings grew up together, spending time at each other's houses, and at school.

This was unusual in much of the United States, as people of different races were frequently required by law to attend different schools, so that White children might have better access to education and "Colored" students deprived of the education that might empower them to advance socially, economically and politically: education is one of culture's most valuable resources. And is a Human Right. In many places, the Lovings would have never gone to school with one another.

Segregation also occurred in neighborhoods, separating Colored people from Whites. This occurred not only by law, but also by covenants (agreements made between buyers and sellers of homes that the home would not be sold to Colored people) as well as by policies of banks and other mortgage lenders, who would not lend money to buy a home to Colored people if they wanted to buy a home in a "White neighborhood." In many places, the Lovings would never have grown up with each other so nearby.

It was also unusual because interracial relationships were illegal in much of the United States, not only the South, at the time. This reflected local beliefs in racism, and the fear that if Colored people were allowed to have relationships with White people, they would endanger the purity and superiority of the White race. However, laws could vary city to city, or county to county: for example, in Colorado, most counties in the Western and Southern half of the State allowed interracial relationships, while many counties in the Eastern and Northern half of the State did not - but even in Colorado, there were exceptions.

Yet the reason why interracial relationships are legal everywhere in the United States, the reason why interracial relationships have become so widely accepted as to allow even an interracial couple to live in the Naval Observatory (which is the Vice President's residence: Vice President Kamala Harris is the daughter of Jamaican and Indian immigrants, and her husband, is of Semitic and White descent), is because of the Lovings.

The Lovings had to fight to win the right for their marriage to be recognized not only in their County, but everywhere they wanted to be. They fought for that right in the Supreme Court. Though their hometown was not racist, their county was: Caroline County, where Central Point is, had its own laws, even if the town of Central Point was integrated.

One of the reasons why they were able to fight was because they had grown up in a town where things were different from surrounding areas, and could see both worlds. This helped them understand the dangers of racist beliefs, and imagine a way of life without them.

Speaking of the lack of racism in their hometown of Central Point, Richard told *Life Magazine* after their victory, "it never was like a lot of other places. It doesn't matter to folks around here...They just want to live and be left alone. That's the way I feel."

If they had not lived where racist laws did not prevent them from falling in love, they could not have imagined a world without these sorts of racist laws preventing them from loving each other wherever they wanted to live or travel. Or a world where anyone might love anyone they wanted to.

Richard had grown up as close friends with Mildred's older brothers and so he was often at their house to visit and play: he was like one of the family. When he grew older, Richard and Mildred later began dating.

They loved each other dearly, and Mildred became pregnant when she was 18 years old. Their son was born in January 1957. By that point, Richard had moved in with Mildred's family to be with her and their son. The couple would eventually have three children together.

Richard and Mildred decided to get married in 1958. At the time, Virginia was one of 24 states where interracial relationships were still illegal: despite the local sentiments of Central Point, the State of Virginia had decided to enact racist laws across its entire State. So in order to get around this, the couple traveled to Washington, D.C. to be married.

Five weeks later, it was not the local police, but County Sheriffs who stormed their home at 2 a.m. on an anonymous tip that someone had broken several racist laws: it was reported that a Colored woman had a baby with a White man, that they were living together, and were apparently married.

The County Sheriff indeed caught the Lovings in the act of breaking the law: they were sleeping together, there was a baby as proof that they had been sleeping together a long time, and when the County Sheriff asked Richard who was sleeping with him, Richard said that she was his wife, and pointed to their marriage license on the wall. The Sheriff said that marriage license was not valid in Virginia and both Richard and Milderd were immediately arrested and booked into jail.

Richard was held for one night, but he was not allowed to bail out his wife. She was kept in jail for nearly a month: racism held it was more illegal for a Colored woman to have a relationship with a White man than for a White man to have a relationship with a Colored woman.

1958: Loving to Fight

Exile from Virginia

Mildred Loving later said, "When my late husband, Richard, and I got married in Washington, D.C. in 1958, it wasn't to make a political statement or start a fight. We were in love, and we wanted to be married."

But they did find that if they wanted to remain married, and raise their children together, they were making a political statement and would have to fight for what their relationship stood for.

The Lovings were charged under Section 20-58 of the Virginia Code, which prohibited interracial couples from being married out of state and then returning to Virginia, and Section 20-59, which classified this kind of interracial marriage as a felony, punishable by a prison sentence of between one and five years.

The evidence and confessions of the couple were indisputable: on January 6, 1959, the Lovings pleaded guilty to "cohabiting as man and wife, against the peace and dignity of the Commonwealth." They were sentenced to one year in prison.

However, the Lovings were able to negotiate a plea bargain with the district attorney and get the prison sentence suspended if they would agree to an exile, and stay out of Virginia for 25 years.

The Lovings moved to Washington, D.C., where they lived for five years. But the separation from their families was too hard. They were alone in a new city, and it was hard for them. They loved each other dearly, but they also loved their families.

Facing prison sentences if they did return, they sent a letter to the U.S. Attorney General Robert F. Kennedy, who referred them to the American Civil Liberties Union (ACLU).

The ACLU provided the Lovings lawyers. The Lovings could not argue they were innocent: they clearly had broken many laws, and were felons. Instead, their lawyers advised the Lovings to argue they should not be punished with prison because Virginia's racist laws violated the couple's equal rights protection provided by the 14th Amendment to the United States Constitution.

So their lawyers filed motions to this effect.

On October 28, 1964, after waiting almost a year for a response to their motion, the ACLU attorneys filed a federal class action lawsuit in the U.S. District Court for the Eastern District of Virginia. This prompted the county court Judge in the case, Leon M. Bazile, to issue a ruling on the long-pending motion to vacate. Echoing Johann Friedrich Blumenbach's 18th-century interpretation of race, Bazile denied the motion with the words:

"Almighty God created the races White, Black, yellow, malay and red, and he placed them on separate continents. And but for the interference with his arrangement there would be no cause for such marriages. The fact that he separated the races shows that he did not intend for the races to mix."

However scientifically unsound, (every continent is ethnically diverse), with this ruling in place, the Lovings could not take their case to the U.S. District Court, but had to first appeal the decision of the Judge to the Virginia Supreme Court: consequently, on January 22, 1965, a three-judge district court panel postponed decision on the federal case while the Lovings appealed Judge Bazile's decision on constitutional grounds to the Virginia Supreme Court.

On March 7, 1966, Virginia Supreme Court Justice Harry L. Carrico (later Chief Justice of the Court) wrote an opinion for the court upholding the constitutionality of the anti interracial marriage statutes. Carrico cited as authority the Virginia Supreme Court's decision in *Naim v. Naim* (1955) and ruled that criminalization of the Lovings' marriage was not a violation of the Equal Protection Clause, because both the White and the non-White spouse were punished equally for interracial marriage.

This was a common line of reasoning that echoed that of the United States Supreme Court in 1883 in *Pace v. Alabama* and has been used to defend all manner of racist laws, ranging from laws preventing Colored races from living in White neighborhoods, to laws protecting Whites from having to serve Colored people in their businesses.

In the case of *Pace v. Alabama* (1883), the U.S. Supreme Court ruled that the conviction of an Alabama couple for interracial relations, affirmed on appeal by the Alabama Supreme Court, did not violate the Fourteenth Amendment. On appeal, the United States Supreme Court ruled that the criminalization of interracial relations was not a violation of the Equal Protection Clause because Whites and non-Whites were punished in equal measure for the offense of engaging in interracial relations. The Court had decided it did not need to weigh the constitutionality of the ban on interracial marriage itself, since the plaintiff, Mr. Pace, had chosen not to appeal that section of the law - as the Lovings now were doing.

However, the Virginia Supreme Court did find the Lovings' sentences to be unconstitutionally vague, ordering that they be resentenced in the Caroline County Circuit Court: this meant they were again possibly facing prison.

The Lovings, still supported by the ACLU, appealed the Virginia Supreme Court's decision to the Supreme Court of the United States, where Virginia was represented by Robert McIlwaine of the state's attorney general's office.

The Supreme Court agreed on December 12, 1966, to accept the case for final review.

The Lovings did not attend the oral arguments in Washington, but one of their lawyers, Bernard S. Cohen, conveyed the personal message he had been given by Richard Loving: "Mr. Cohen, tell the Court I love my wife, and it is just unfair that I can't live with her in Virginia."

Precedents: the History of Challenging Interracial Marriage Laws

Before the Lovings fought for their rights, there had been several other couples who had fought for their rights in interracial relationships.

Within the state of Virginia, on October 3, 1878, in *Kinney v. The Commonwealth*, the Supreme Court of Virginia ruled that the marriage legalized in Washington, D.C. between Andrew Kinney, a Black man, and Mahala Miller, a White woman, was invalid in Virginia. This was a loss that echoed what happened to the Lovings: but unlike the Lovigns, Kinney and Miller did not appeal this and fight for their rights in the U.S. Supreme Court.

In *Kirby v. Kirby* (1921), Joe R. Kirby asked the state of Arizona for an annulment of his marriage. He argued that his marriage was invalid because his wife was of "negro" descent, thus violating the state's interracial marriage laws. The Arizona Supreme Court agreed with Mr. Kirby, and decided Mayellen Kirby was in fact of "negro" descent and of Colored race by examining her physical characteristics. Therefore, they granted Joe R. Kirby's annulment.

In the Monks case (*Estate of Monks*, 4. Civ. 2835, Records of California Court of Appeals, Fourth district), the Superior Court of San Diego County in 1939 decided to invalidate the marriage of Marie Antoinette and Allan Monks because she was deemed to have "one eighth negro blood." The court case involved a legal challenge over the conflicting wills that had been left by the late Allan Monks; an old one in favor of a friend named Ida Lee, and a newer one in favor of his wife. Lee's lawyers argued that the marriage, which had taken place in Arizona, was invalid under Arizona state law because Marie Antoinette was "a Negro" and Alan was White.

In this case, Marie Monks appeared White. However, a surgeon was hired as an expert witness and described anatomical features he argued proved that she was in fact partially Black. In response, an anthropologist and a biologist were hired as expert witnesses, and they said it was impossible to tell a person's race from physical characteristics, and that race was not scientifically defined, that there was only one human race. The Judge chose to ignore the scientists, and follow the conclusions of the surgeon, determining that she was in fact Colored.

Monks then challenged the Arizona racist law itself, taking her case to the California Court of Appeals, Fourth District. Monks' lawyers pointed out that the anti interracial marriage law effectively prohibited Monks as a mixed-race person from marrying anyone: "As such, she is prohibited from marrying a negro or any descendant of a negro, a Mongolian or an Indian, a Malay or a Hindu, or any descendants of any of them. Likewise … as a descendant of a negro she is prohibited from marrying a Caucasian or a descendant of a Caucasian." This, they argued unfairly deprived her of the right to marry, and was therefore an unconstitutional constraint on her liberty.

However, the court dismissed this argument as inapplicable, because the case presented involved not two mixed-race spouses but a mixed-race and a White spouse, and that their duty was to defend the White spouse from marriage to a Colored woman: "Under the facts presented the appellant does not have the benefit of assailing the validity of the statute." Dismissing

Monks' appeal in 1942, the United States Supreme Court refused to reopen the issue.

The turning point came with *Perez v. Sharp* (1948), also known as *Perez v. Lippold.* In *Perez,* the Supreme Court of California recognized that bans on interracial marriage violated the Fourteenth Amendment of the Federal Constitution.

This in turn gave hope to the Lovings that they might prevail at the U.S. Supreme Court against the State of Virginia.

1967: Free Lovings

Victory

On June 12, 1967, the Supreme Court issued a unanimous 9-0 decision in favor of the Lovings that overturned their criminal convictions and struck down Virginia's anti interracial marriage law. The Court's opinion was written by chief justice Earl Warren, and all the justices joined it.

The Court first addressed whether Virginia's Racial Integrity Act violated the Fourteenth Amendment's Equal Protection Clause, which reads: "nor shall any State ... deny to any person within its jurisdiction the equal protection of the laws."

The U.S. Supreme Court observed Virginia officials had argued that the Act did not violate the Equal Protection Clause because it "equally burdened" both Whites and non-Whites, since the punishment for violating the statute was the same regardless of the offender's race; for example, a White person who married a Black person was subject to the same penalties as a Black person who married a White person.

To this, the U.S. Supreme Court said that because citizens were defined according to their ancestry, they could not be equal: there was observed to be some kind of difference between them. If they were truly equal, if they were all human, there would be no way to define a marriage as interracial at all: it would be no different than a marriage between people of different White ancestry marrying, or people of different Colored ancestry marrying. All people were equals, which meant all people were the same. The State of Virginia's argument suggested that the law saw two kinds of people: White people, and Colored people, and therefore Virginian racist law was invalid. All racist laws were invalid.

"There can be no question but that Virginia's miscegenation statutes rest solely upon distinctions drawn according to race. The statutes proscribe generally accepted conduct if engaged in by members of different races. Over the years, this Court has consistently repudiated "[d]istinctions between citizens solely because of their ancestry" as being "odious to a free people whose institutions are founded upon the doctrine of equality." At the very least, the Equal Protection Clause demands that racial classifications, especially suspect in criminal statutes, be subjected to the "most rigid scrutiny."
– *Loving*, 388 U.S. at 11 (alteration in original) (citations omitted).

The U.S. Supreme Court concluded that Virginia's Act had no discernible purpose other than "invidious racial discrimination" that was designed to "maintain White Supremacy." The Court therefore ruled that the Act violated the Equal Protection Clause.

*"There is patently no legitimate overriding purpose
independent of invidious racial discrimination which justifies
this classification. The fact that Virginia prohibits only interracial
marriages involving White persons demonstrates that the racial
classifications must stand on their own justification, as
measures designed to maintain White Supremacy. We have
consistently denied the constitutionality of measures which
restrict the rights of citizens on account of race. There can be
no doubt that restricting the freedom to marry solely because
of racial classifications violates the central meaning of the Equal
Protection Clause."*
– *Loving*, 388 U.S. at 11-12.

The U.S. Supreme Court ended its opinion with a short
section holding that Virginia's Racial Integrity Act also violated
the Fourteenth Amendment's Due Process Clause: the Court said
that the freedom to marry is a fundamental constitutional right,
and it held that depriving Americans of it on an arbitrary basis
such as race was unconstitutional.

*"These statutes also deprive the Lovings of liberty without
due process of law in violation of the Due Process Clause of the
Fourteenth Amendment. The freedom to marry has long been*

recognized as one of the vital personal rights essential to the orderly pursuit of happiness by free men.

Marriage is one of the "basic civil rights of man," fundamental to our very existence and survival. To deny this fundamental freedom on so unsupportable a basis as the racial classifications embodied in these statutes, classifications so directly subversive of the principle of equality at the heart of the Fourteenth Amendment, is surely to deprive all the State's citizens of liberty without due process of law."

— *Loving*, 388 U.S. at 12 (citations omitted).

Happily Ever After...Eventually

Despite the Supreme Court's decision, anti interracial marriage laws remained on the books in several states, although the decision had made them unenforceable. State judges in Alabama continued to enforce its anti interracial marriage statute until 1970, when the Nixon administration obtained a ruling from a U.S. District Court in *United States v. Brittain*.

In 2000, Alabama became the last state to adapt its laws to the Supreme Court's decision, when 60% of voters endorsed a constitutional amendment, Amendment 2, that removed anti interracial marriage language from the state constitution.

Interracial Marriage Rate Increased

After Loving v. Virginia, the number of interracial marriages continued to increase across the United States. However, they are still relatively rare in the South. In Georgia, the number of interracial marriages per year increased from 21 in 1967 to 115 in 1970. Comparatively, at the national level, 0.4% of marriages were interracial in 1960, 2.0% in 1980, 12% in 2013, and 16% in 2015, almost 50 years after Loving.

Same Sex Marriage

Loving v. Virginia was eventually used to justify same sex marriage.

In *Hernandez v. Robles* (2006), the majority opinion of the New York Court of Appeals - New York State's highest court - declined to rely on the *Loving* case when deciding whether a right to same-sex marriage existed, holding that "the historical background of Loving is different from the history underlying this case." This opened the debate on whether *Loving* could be applied to same sex marriage.

A counterargument was made in the 2010 federal district court decision in *Perry v. Schwarzenegger*, which overturned California's Proposition 8 restricting marriage to opposite-sex couples. There, Judge Vaughn R. Walker cited *Loving v. Virginia* as support to conclude that "the [constitutional] right to marry protects an individual's choice of marital partner regardless of gender." On narrower grounds, the 9th Circuit Court of Appeals affirmed this understanding.

Up until 2014, five U.S. Courts of Appeals considered the constitutionality of state bans on same-sex marriage. In doing so they interpreted or used the Loving ruling differently:

The Fourth and Tenth Circuits used *Loving* along with other cases like *Zablocki v. Redhail* and *Turner v. Safley* to demonstrate that the U.S. Supreme Court has recognized a "fundamental right to marry" that a state cannot restrict unless it meets the court's "heightened scrutiny" standard. Using that standard, both courts struck down state bans on same-sex marriage.

Two other courts of appeals, the Seventh and Ninth Circuits, struck down state bans on the basis of a different line of argument. Instead of "fundamental rights" analysis, they reviewed bans on same-sex marriage as discrimination on the basis of sexual orientation. The former cited Loving to demonstrate that the Supreme Court did not accept tradition as a justification for limiting access to marriage. The latter cited Loving as quoted in *United States v. Windsor* on the question of federalism: "state laws defining or regulating marriage, of course, must respect the constitutional rights of persons."

The only Court of Appeals to uphold state bans on same-sex marriage, the Sixth Circuit, said that when the *Loving* decision discussed marriage it was referring only to marriage between persons of the opposite sex. Despite no reference to sexual orientation being made in the decision.

In *Obergefell v. Hodges* (2015), the Supreme Court invoked Loving, among other cases, as precedent for its holding that states are required to allow same-sex marriages under both the Equal Protection Clause and the Due Process Clause of the Constitution. The court's decision in Obergefell cited Loving nearly a dozen times, and was based on the same principles – equality and an unenumerated right to marriage. During oral argument, the eventual author of the majority opinion, Justice Anthony Kennedy, noted that the ruling holding racial segregation unconstitutional and the ruling holding bans on interracial marriage unconstitutional (*Brown v. Board of Education* in 1954 and *Loving v. Virginia* in 1967) were made about 13 years apart, much like the ruling holding bans on same-sex sexual activity unconstitutional and the eventual ruling holding bans on same-sex marriage unconstitutional (*Lawrence v. Texas* in 2003 and *Obergefell v. Hodges* in 2015).

The Loving Legacy

Sadly, Richard Loving was killed by a drunk driver in 1975, seven years after the Supreme Court ruling. Mildred was injured but survived the crash.

In June 2007, on the 40th anniversary of the Supreme Court's decision in Loving, Mildred Loving issued the following statement:

"My generation was bitterly divided over something that should have been so clear and right. The majority believed that what the judge said, that it was God's plan to keep people apart, and that government should discriminate against people in love. But I have lived long enough now to see big changes. The older generation's fears and prejudices have given way, and today's young people realize that if someone loves someone they have a right to marry.

Surrounded as I am now by wonderful children and grandchildren, not a day goes by that I don't think of Richard and our love, our right to marry, and how much it meant to me to have that freedom to marry the person precious to me, even if others thought he was the "wrong kind of person" for me to marry. I believe all Americans, no matter their race, no matter their sex, no matter their sexual orientation, should have that same freedom to marry. Government has no business imposing some people's religious beliefs over others. Especially if it denies people's civil rights.

I am still not a political person, but I am proud that Richard's and my name is on a court case that can help reinforce the love, the commitment, the fairness, and the family that so many people, Black or White, young or old, gay or straight seek in life. I support the freedom to marry for all. That's what Loving, and loving, are all about."

Appendix: the United Nations Declaration of Human Rights

There is some concern today that Loving may be overturned by the Supreme Court. However, marriage is a fundamental right guaranteed not only by the U.S. Constitution as interpreted by the Supreme Court, but is explicitly protected by the Declaration of Human Rights: marriage is a fundamental right by Article 16 of the Declaration of Human Rights, which the United States agreed to abide by and uphold through treaty.

*This Declaration is one which **all people in the United States may appeal for protection** for their fundamental rights, and as such, there is no better conclusion to this book than to include it in appendix.*

Preamble

Whereas recognition of the inherent dignity and of the equal and inalienable rights of all members of the human family is the foundation of freedom, justice and peace in the world,

Whereas disregard and contempt for human rights have resulted in barbarous acts which have outraged the conscience of mankind, and the advent of a world in which human beings shall enjoy freedom of speech and belief and freedom from fear and want has been proclaimed as the highest aspiration of the common people,

Whereas it is essential, if man is not to be compelled to have recourse, as a last resort, to rebellion against tyranny and oppression, that human rights should be protected by the rule of law,

Whereas it is essential to promote the development of friendly relations between nations,

Whereas the peoples of the United Nations have in the Charter reaffirmed their faith in fundamental human rights, in the dignity and worth of the human person and in the equal rights of men and women and have determined to promote social progress and better standards of life in larger freedom,

Whereas Member States have pledged themselves to achieve, in co-operation with the United Nations, the promotion of universal respect for and observance of human rights and fundamental freedoms,

Whereas a common understanding of these rights and freedoms is of the greatest importance for the full realization of this pledge,

Now, therefore,

The General Assembly,

Proclaims this Universal Declaration of Human Rights as a common standard of achievement for all peoples and all nations, to the end that every individual and every organ of society, keeping this Declaration constantly in mind, shall strive by teaching and education to promote respect for these rights and freedoms and by progressive measures, national and international, to secure their universal and effective recognition and observance, both among the peoples of Member States themselves and among the peoples of territories under their jurisdiction.

Article 1

All human beings are born free and equal in dignity and rights. They are endowed with reason and conscience and should act towards one another in a spirit of brotherhood.

Article 2

Everyone is entitled to all the rights and freedoms set forth in this Declaration, without distinction of any kind, such as race, colour, sex, language, religion, political or other opinion, national or social origin, property, birth or other status. Furthermore, no distinction shall be made on the basis of the political, jurisdictional or international status of the country or territory to which a person belongs, whether it be independent, trust, non-self-governing or under any other limitation of sovereignty.

Article 3

Everyone has the right to life, liberty and security of person.

Article 4

No one shall be held in slavery or servitude; slavery and the slave trade shall be prohibited in all their forms.

Article 5

No one shall be subjected to torture or to cruel, inhuman or degrading treatment or punishment.

Article 6

Everyone has the right to recognition everywhere as a person before the law.

Article 7

All are equal before the law and are entitled without any discrimination to equal protection of the law. All are entitled to equal protection against any discrimination in violation of this Declaration and against any incitement to such discrimination.

Article 8

Everyone has the right to an effective remedy by the competent national tribunals for acts violating the fundamental rights granted him by the constitution or by law.

Article 9

No one shall be subjected to arbitrary arrest, detention or exile.

Article 10

Everyone is entitled in full equality to a fair and public hearing by an independent and impartial tribunal, in the determination of his rights and obligations and of any criminal charge against him.

Article 11

Everyone charged with a penal offence has the right to be presumed innocent until proved guilty according to law in a public trial at which he has had all the guarantees necessary for his defence.

No one shall be held guilty of any penal offence on account of any act or omission which did not constitute a penal offence, under national or international law, at the time when it was committed. Nor shall a heavier penalty be imposed than the one that was applicable at the time the penal offence was committed.

Article 12

No one shall be subjected to arbitrary interference with his privacy, family, home or correspondence, nor to attacks upon his honour and reputation. Everyone has the right to the protection of the law against such interference or attacks.

Article 13

Everyone has the right to freedom of movement and residence within the borders of each state.

Everyone has the right to leave any country, including his own, and to return to his country.

Article 14

Everyone has the right to seek and to enjoy in other countries asylum from persecution.

This right may not be invoked in the case of prosecutions genuinely arising from non-political crimes or from acts contrary to the purposes and principles of the United Nations.

Article 15

Everyone has the right to a nationality.

No one shall be arbitrarily deprived of his nationality nor denied the right to change his nationality.

Article 16

Men and women of full age, without any limitation due to race, nationality or religion, have the right to marry and to found a family. They are entitled to equal rights as to marriage, during marriage and at its dissolution.

Marriage shall be entered into only with the free and full consent of the intending spouses.

The family is the natural and fundamental group unit of society and is entitled to protection by society and the State.

Article 17

Everyone has the right to own property alone as well as in association with others.

No one shall be arbitrarily deprived of his property.

Article 18

Everyone has the right to freedom of thought, conscience and religion; this right includes freedom to change his religion or belief, and freedom, either alone or in community with others and in public or private, to manifest his religion or belief in teaching, practice, worship and observance.

Article 19

Everyone has the right to freedom of opinion and expression; this right includes freedom to hold opinions without interference and to seek, receive and impart information and ideas through any media and regardless of frontiers.

Article 20

Everyone has the right to freedom of peaceful assembly and association.

No one may be compelled to belong to an association.

Article 21

Everyone has the right to take part in the government of his country, directly or through freely chosen representatives.

Everyone has the right of equal access to public service in his country.

The will of the people shall be the basis of the authority of government; this will shall be expressed in periodic and genuine elections which shall be by universal and equal suffrage and shall be held by secret vote or by equivalent free voting procedures.

Article 22

Everyone, as a member of society, has the right to social security and is entitled to realization, through national effort and international co-operation and in accordance with the organization and resources of each State, of the economic, social and cultural rights indispensable for his dignity and the free development of his personality.

Article 23

Everyone has the right to work, to free choice of employment, to just and favourable conditions of work and to protection against unemployment.

Everyone, without any discrimination, has the right to equal pay for equal work.

Everyone who works has the right to just and favourable remuneration ensuring for himself and his family an existence worthy of human dignity, and supplemented, if necessary, by other means of social protection.

Everyone has the right to form and to join trade unions for the protection of his interests.

Article 24

Everyone has the right to rest and leisure, including reasonable limitation of working hours and periodic holidays with pay.

Article 25

Everyone has the right to a standard of living adequate for the health and well-being of himself and of his family, including food, clothing, housing and medical care and necessary social services, and the right to security in the event of unemployment, sickness, disability, widowhood, old age or other lack of livelihood in circumstances beyond his control.

Motherhood and childhood are entitled to special care and assistance. All children, whether born in or out of wedlock, shall enjoy the same social protection.

Article 26

Everyone has the right to education. Education shall be free, at least in the elementary and fundamental stages. Elementary education shall be compulsory. Technical and professional education shall be made generally available and higher education shall be equally accessible to all on the basis of merit.

Education shall be directed to the full development of the human personality and to the strengthening of respect for human rights and fundamental freedoms. It shall promote understanding, tolerance and friendship among all nations, racial or religious groups, and shall further the activities of the United Nations for the maintenance of peace.

Parents have a prior right to choose the kind of education that shall be given to their children.

Article 27

Everyone has the right freely to participate in the cultural life of the community, to enjoy the arts and to share in scientific advancement and its benefits.

Everyone has the right to the protection of the moral and material interests resulting from any scientific, literary or artistic production of which he is the author.

Article 28

Everyone is entitled to a social and international order in which the rights and freedoms set forth in this Declaration can be fully realized.

Article 29

Everyone has duties to the community in which alone the free and full development of his personality is possible.

In the exercise of his rights and freedoms, everyone shall be subject only to such limitations as are determined by law solely for the purpose of securing due recognition and respect for the rights and freedoms of others and of meeting the just requirements of morality, public order and the general welfare in a democratic society.

These rights and freedoms may in no case be exercised contrary to the purposes and principles of the United Nations.

Article 30

Nothing in this Declaration may be interpreted as implying for any State, group or person any right to engage in any activity or to perform any act aimed at the destruction of any of the rights and freedoms set forth herein.